UNBREAKABLE

Poetry for the unshakeable souls

Rohini Linda

BookLeaf Publishing

India | USA | UK

Made with ❤ on the BookLeaf Publishing Platform
www.bookleafpub.in
www.bookleafpub.com

Dedication

This Piece of work is a testimony of my love for my lovely child ,my soulmate "Amor"

The strong and kind woman that you will become and find wisdom through the words in this book.

~ Lots of love from "MOM"

Preface

I choose to be silent for my strength lies in my
soul,
I do not live to prove my existence but to write
poems that inspire millions of my kinds.
Who take the courage to tread the darkness and
bring themselves to light.

~

I hope this book finds anybody who needs guidance in difficult and hard times, the ones who are grappled by fear at the crossroads in their life's journey where moving forward seems impossible and loneliness sets in.

I am certain that these words will resonate and bring insights through the wisdom I gained during my difficult times and found inner strength through knowing that I am whole and complete and that assurance gave me enough strength to navigate through my life one day at a time.whatever you may be going through is just a passing phase. Just hang on there and take one day at a time. Surrender, self care and self love are the most important pillars to drag you out of this. Be open and let your soul guide you to your own real self.

I urge you to also acknowledge your feelings as your proceed to read for they are part of your shadows that lie dormant in the corner of your mind, without judgement acknowledge them as they emerge. These feelings have long been trying to be seen and heard to be fully felt and released creating new ones to emerge. As empaths and sensitive people , especially women and souls who resonate more with their femininity, we suppress ourselves to make others feel more comfortable around us. we need to reclaim the parts that we hide and take up space and hold safe boundaries to live and thrive.

The most difficult times of our lives are also the most remarkable turning point in time to deconstruct all our illusions and egoistic desires and to find the real self that relentlessly is pushed into our shadows of the mind.It is very important to connect to those aspects and become whole and complete through integration.

Since, I am a tarot card reader and astrologer by profession,I understand these feelings and emotions through my work and personal experiences. However I felt guided to write it and present in the form of poetry ,the language of the soul.

Since in this new age, everything is searchable and everyone can research to find knowledge through technology and internet to empower their minds. The soul has a language of its own and I could express through my poetry is what I believe is a blessing that I have been bestowed upon.

The emotions expressed in the poems are resonances that will be guidelines and help in navigating life with surrender and knowing that universe is always supportive of us.
Crisis and moments of breakdown often happens when we bottle up our emotions and do not express and have pushed aside our own desire to create a life but lived by the norms of society and try to fit into boxes of expectations which do not serve us.

Some poems are a window to the soul and account for memories and situations faced, some define how we can feel stuck in the constructs of our mind, some have stories of parts of me that i discovered during my journey and met people I resonated with at my deepest level.

All of these are only accounts of feelings and we are powerful creators of change and as per my experience , when i started looking into them closely and embarked on my healing journey , I realised that a soul is unbreakable and unshakeable at its core.

We must always follow our heart for it knows the best and self love and compassion can lead us to become the most authentic version and true to ourself.

Acknowledgements

I wish to acknowledge the seen and unseen forces of nature that inspired me to write this book . I want to pay gratitude to all my small and big moments of life that helped me gain wisdom and my ancestors who are always there to guide and support me.

1. Untold memories

My untold memories hold the key to my pain.
The efforts that were never acknowledged
The love that was never reciprocated
The desires that were never fulfilled
The respect that was never received
The feelings that were never expressed
For I believed in the unspoken,
not knowing that even i was not hearing them,
until the day I started to hear them in myself again.

~ Realisations by Rohini

2. Strength

*I was raised by the queens, the mortal goddesses that
contained fire in their bellies
and sea of love in their hearts.
The ferals who carried air of rage in their hairlocks,
their breath whispered songs of wisdom that can create
sparks.
The calmness in their footsteps and the strength in their
hands
that nurtured my soul into the spirit that I guard.
I owe my being to my ancestry, to the women who
raised me,
the one who birthed me and to the one I brought to life
and am meant to raise as my child.*

~ Realisations by Rohini

3. Thoughts

As I started walking with my thoughts they started
nudging me softly.
I ran to catch the ones that spoke more calmly .
The ones that were left behind were the ones that would
never make into my reality.
Witnessing my own unfolding
with every breath and thoughts that run deep into my
soul,
found a version of myself that I never though existed
until I turned in to find myself in a universe that holds
my thoughts and turns into actuality.

~ Realisations by Rohini

4. Broken dreams

The shards of my broken dreams pain in my eyes,
the tears that flow endlessly
scream stories of unspoken lies.
Sleep runs far away and
anxiety engulfs my soul
trying to hide in the darkest corner of my mind.

~ Realisations by Rohini

5. Hopeless

Sometimes in life we do not know where we are ,
Feeling stuck in memories as grief never seems to
subside
with uncertainty of no future in sight.
All we have is now which is the present moment,
hence called the gift of time.
Still the memories deceive and illusions of future entice.
I look into it all at once through my newfound eyes.
The one that sparkles with hope and smile,
for this moment will define my future as past is left
behind
and create my life every second with love and a light
that I choose to shine.

~Realisations by Rohini

6. Pain

The shards of broken memoirs of time haunts me each day,
to unravel the grief that I chose to to bury in the depths of the archives of my soul,
of unresolved experiences that seep now into my life,
as past cannot be brought back and letting go seems impossible,
for the soul to keep its peace a poet must create ,
masterpieces of invisible pain that lingers as poems and find no place to hide.

~ Realisations by Rohini

7. Prayers

There are times when days feel longer to bear and nights with unfathomable darkness that never seem to see the light.
The tunnel of endless shadows seems never ending and the fear that does not subside.
I promise myself to remain in my strength for that's all I have known .
The one that comes from the abyss of my soul from the prayers that I recited my entire life.

~ Realisations by Rohini

8. The call

When your soul is knocking the doors of your heart
answer the call, for what you do not know what you
may be opening up to,
a version of you that was hidden in your shadows has
come to meet you
from the depths of the ashes of your past.
The one you hide and deny will show itself with
a storm to be embraced with love and kindness
that it always deserved to be accepted and stay forever in
your heart.

~ Realisations by Rohini

9. Success

I want to break all the barriers and
the invisible walls of expectations that hold my kind.
For the real expression of self that we hold is a gift from
the divine.
As I walked on fire and fought with my inner demons
that contrived.
I want you to know they are just the constructs of the
mind.
Do not buy the stories of how success should materialise
as you have a path
carved especially and designed for you to realise.

~ Realisations by Rohini

10. Journaling

My heart feels at ease as I pen down my story into words of grace.
They are messages for the ones who need it most in times of
distress and pain. when nobody can understand and all explanations fail,
the wisdom we can resonate with are the ones that keep us sane.
Keep writing all your feelings as they are looking for a release.
Burn them into ashes that turn into forgotten memories down the lane.

~ Realisations by Rohini

11. Mirrors

I do not meet people with their faces now ,
I meet them at the depth of their soul and the shadows
that they hide.
I try to understand now and feel the overwhelm ,
the thoughts , the pain , the emotions, the heartache and
the feelings that reside.
I hold a mirror and space for them to decide to break the
mirror or look deep inside.
I was so scared of being a mirror at first but now I accept
my fate
for we all are mirrors that capture the unseen shadows
for each other to be seen and heard.
I look at the mirrors now with curious eyes, In search of
answers that I always yearned to find.

~ Realisations by Rohini

12. Connections

I connect with poets ,the artists and writers ,
the ones who bring my thoughts alive.
The ones that I hold in my mind but cannot bring out to
thrive.
Some expressions that are held in a corner of my mind
that have not found a way to be penned down ,
but I resonate with each word and feel it as it's mine.
The soulmates of the other world, the messengers in this
lifetime.
The mirrors to my soul who bring out the hidden parts of
me to light.
In a language that flows and shines the part of me that
was yearning to fight.
Happiness and peace dwells in those moments
in a world where I live and find chaos in everyday life.

~ Realisations by Rohini

13. Anger

The discomfort that I feel when my boundaries have
been ignored.
The rage, the burning sensation I feel is just
the helplessness that I feel
of sadness and the disappointment of not being
reciprocated
of the respect that I always poured.
Emptiness comes from overgiving and anger when over
expecting from unmet needs.
I therefore feel the urge to set boundaries so concrete
that can hold me from over giving
and understand the message that my anger brings to
listen and pay heed.

~ Realisations by Rohini

14. Imaginations

We are all in our stories, peeping through the shadows
that keep prompting to dig into our quarries.
In some we are victims and in some victorious .
ones where we are wounded kids and in some warriors
of light.
In some we are victims and in some warriors of light.
In some the maiden in distress and warriors and the
knights.
Some bring to me bouts of depression and anxiety
and some are capable of bringing so much delight.
The ones that I love the most are the ones that come
from my own light ,
with wisdom as deep as ocean and
courage to soar as a bird taking a flight.
But once I sit at home and sip my tea,
I see how imaginative i can be.
If they do not serve me in reality they do not deserve to
be in my life
for they can only be in moments of awareness and to
keep me in flight or fight.

Yet a small part of me is so romantic ,
that loves to dwell in all my fantasies and write poems to
bring my characters to sprite.

~ Realisations by Rohini

15. Home

My home is a space in my mind.
The place that makes me feel at peace,
the one that smells of lavender, sage, incense of jasmine
and candles that warm my hearth.
A sanctuary that I built with long baths and days of
journaling my thoughts.
Meditating with crystals to connect to energies
to find discernment and reading books to find what I
want.
The practices of my ancestors and the ones that I learnt
in this lifetime.
The connection to nature, the earth, the moon and the
stars.
Have all brought me closer to the one I always wanted to
find.

~ Realisations by Rohini

16. Artists

*The world is a beautiful canvas and we all are the artists,
the souls with their each distinct story and unique
colours to fill in
with paintings that bring emotions into reality.
Some drawings are sad and some miserable but hide
tremendous courage and
determination to rise in magnanimity
some are paintings of old memories and happiness that
promise to make us smile till eternity.
some portraits tell tales of struggles and unmet desires
and fears experienced through tragedy.
Yet each of them is important to experience life in its
entirety.*

~ Realisations by Rohini

17. Old soul

*I grieve the unseen and unfelt, the places I wanted to live
in.
The friendships that I could not experience,
the feelings of love that I could not express and many
more that falls in the grey of life.
As these are spaces that fall in between of the feelings
that I witness and find myself in strife.
Life moves and sometimes I flow and sometimes I am
stuck in a reef.
Being an old soul is not easy for the thoughts are stormy
and deep.
When it rains heavily and clouds try to sink into me I
freeze and fall asleep.*

~ Realisations by Rohini

18. Divine Feminine

*There are women around us ,The prayers of thousand
ancestors,
the cycle breakers, the warriors of the night,
divine feminine wisdom embodied into flesh,
the ones that may seem ordinary but hold immense
promise of light.
Not known by what they do but the ones who reclaim
their power by being who they are.
Nobody seems to see them as they often hide in plain
sight.
They are wrapped as feelings of peace and are blessings
that you may feel only when you are in their shine.
women are powerful manifestors and they embody the
channel to the divine.*

~ Realisations by Rohini

19. Tribe

The women of change are here, to birth a new era of
hope in every sphere.
Looking relentlessly for knowledge and wisdom
and uprooting all belief system that is here.
Hunting day and night for the fire that can bring light to
humanity
and free the caged souls out of their naivety.
The ones who fold their hands in prayers,
the ones who kneel down for blessings and
the ones who meditate to receive messages of their
ancestry.
To serve ,to heal, to create peace and to bring endless
positivity.

~ Realisations by Rohini

20. Millennial mom

Living as a millennial that seems have seen it all,
still cannot connect to any of it as the mind seems so
small.
In a space that is rapidly expanding ,
transforming and changing with no traces of vocabulary
that finds a resonance to my brain.
The Genz , the Gen alpha and some others that are next
in chain.
I dread all the words and smirks,
the giggles and blanks that creates a trench so deep,
I fear I might fall and die.
The words that are said so casually
have meanings that shame me and shake me from inside

,

makes me think am I so sensitive
or is the world becoming a place where i cannot survive.

~ Realisations by Rohini

21. Transformation

*I tried to find reasons to stay in relationships that
expired long back,
the uncomfortable conversations with no meanings and
resonance and filled them with small talk.
Tried holding on to finding the ambience by requesting
meetings
and trying to find familiarity in spaces that have no
significance.
The old self is dying and yet clinging to me when new
one birthing is still confusing.
I take small steps to my newness as I let the older one
drift away.
Deep down I know the ones who are meant to stay
forever ,
as they are the ones I can never lose,
The soulmates ,the lovers who are always there a part of
the journey of growth
and are my witnesses that I choose.*

~ Realisations by Rohini

22. Uncovering

Every time I would break, I unlocked something
magnificent in me.
An artist, a poet , a healer and that makes me think.
Breaking is just a part of losing the old, for the old is a
covering.
that covers the hidden truth of my being .
I decided to break free from the inside and unlock all
parts of me.
By making a choice to heal and
create the most beautiful masterpiece that I was destined
to be.

~ Realisations by Rohini

23. Suicide

I never thought betraying myself will cost me my life,
when two steps away I took at the edge of taking a dive.
I chose to live and sacrifice my old in that moment to
understand
that the purpose of life is not in dying for someone but
to live and revive.
I live to tell tales of courage and inspire others to decide
that life
will always be uncertain but with will and choices we
can always thrive.

~ Realisations by Rohini

24. Warrior

I became numb to my pain and problems I denied.
But my soul is a warrior within that does not align.
It started a war inside me only for me to realise.
The fire that I hold within cannot subside.
I started listening to the wisdom that I now imbibe.
My pains are my allies and my problems the pathways
that are leading me to my purpose and find meaning to
my life.

~ Realisations by Rohini

25. Awakening

I have read several books and tried all the tricks ,
The ones that guide you to become the best with
following the ten easy steps to repair.
I could not follow even one for my soul just could not
align, feeling shock and despair .
The awakening comes with a cost that cannot be
simplified,
The loss, the pain , the malice that cannot be justified.
yet the path demand you to move ahead and reclaim
yourself
and be the best version that you are meant to be can
never be satisfied.

~ Realisations by Rohini

26. Empath

I follow the rhythm of my heart,
and the story that flashes in front of my eyes.
The unseen visions that once scared me ,
have now become my guides.
I heard messages from unseen realms,
deemed myself insane and naive.
I owned myself and resonated with my voice,
to bring forth the unique gift that
now I embrace and call myself wise.
For sensitivity is a gift of the chosen ones
to build a new world where infinite possibilities reside.

~ Realisations by Rohini

27. Reclaim

I tried becoming and conforming to what I never was
to find, that love and admiration in the eyes of
others and the respect that was denied.
I started to abandon my voice and started shrinking to
make others shine.
For my light blinded the eyes
that were never as kind as mine.
I started wearing a mask that was stern and not so nice,
to protect my light,
as it was so exhausting to carry my smile.
Isolating from the world that was pretending to be what
they never were
but showing it to me behind .
Shocked as I was to find this duality within my own
mind.
I decided I will be real and as authentic as I shine ,
to find my tribe and live freely for the world to feel as if
it's mine.

~ Realisations by Rohini

28. The Lesson

*My child is a living manifestation of my shadows of
disgrace.
The parts of my angry self and the rebel that I could not
brace.
She shows me each day that its ok to take up space and
show up all emotions
and reclaim them at her own pace.
I now bow down to the lesson and wilfully embrace.
The moments that steer me to accept myself and direct
me to find balance and grace.*

~ Realisations by Rohini

www.ingramcontent.com/pod-product-compliance
Lightning Source LLC
LaVergne TN
LVHW021313200726
843509LV00012B/1904